TIME FOR KIDS READERS

WORLD LANDMARKS

by Susan Ring

**Harcourt**

Orlando   Austin   Chicago   New York   Toronto   London   San Diego

Visit *The Learning Site!*
www.harcourtschool.com

A landmark is something that makes us think of one certain place. It can be a building, a bridge, or even a mountain. Whatever the landmark might be, it is one of a kind.

More than 42 million cars and trucks crossed the Golden Gate Bridge in 2001.

There are many bridges in the United States. But when you see this one, with its bright red color, you know you are in San Francisco. The Golden Gate Bridge is one of the most famous bridges in the world.

This building is the Leaning Tower of Pisa in Italy. Some wonder how much more it will lean before it tips over. Recently people worked to make sure that the tower will not tip over.

The tower leans because it was built on soft soil. No one will set the tower straight all the way, because it has become famous for leaning. Visitors come from all over the world to see it.

Workers started building the Tower of Pisa in 1173. It took almost 200 years to finish it.

These beautiful domes rising into the sky are part of
the Taj Mahal in India. It was built by a ruler of
India more than 300 years ago.
He built it to honor his wife
after she died. With its marble
and gemstones, it is one
of the most beautiful
buildings in the world.

It took 22 years and more than 20,000 workers to build the Taj Mahal.

Did you know that a "lost city" could also be a landmark? Machu Picchu was a city built by the Incas, high in the mountains of Peru. It was uncovered about 100 years ago. There is no other place like it anywhere.

There are many temples, houses, and palaces on Machu Picchu.

A landmark doesn't have to be built by people. Mount Kilimanjaro is the highest mountain peak in Africa. It has its own special shape and stands alone as it towers over the African plains.

In Swahili, the word Kilimanjaro means "the mountain that glitters."